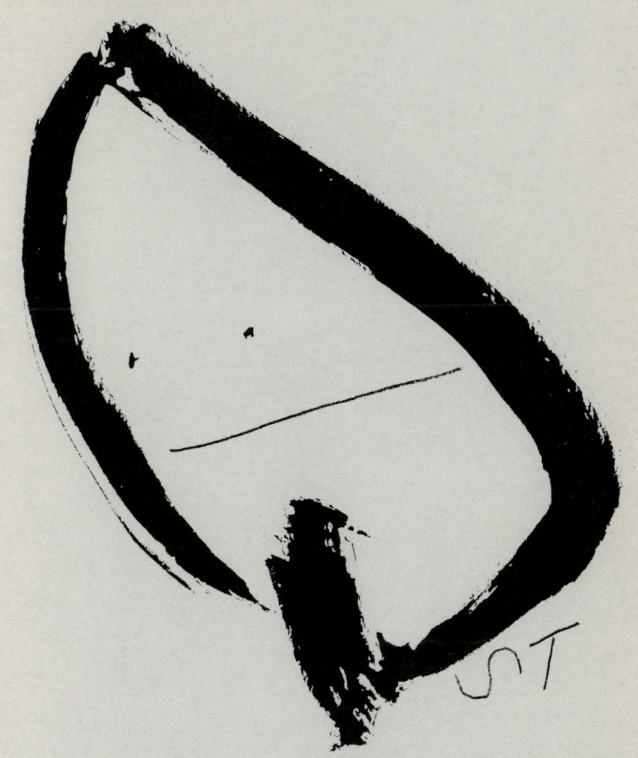

THE SHINO SUITE

sansei poetry
by ronald tanaka

志野ぽえむ

THE SHINO SUITE
Opus 2

by Ronald Tanaka

ACKNOWLEDGMENTS

Library of Congress Catalog Card No. 80-66987
ISBN 0-912678-46-1

Copyright © 1981 Ronald Tanaka

Publication of this book is made possible, in part, by a Small Press
Grant from the National Endowment for the Arts

Greenfield Review Chapbook #46

The Greenfield Review Press
Greenfield Center, NY 12833

to be read in a
single sitting

for Jesse Hiraoka

'People in this world look at things mistakenly, and think that what they do not understand must be the void. This is not the void. This is bewilderment.'

—Miyamoto Musashi
A BOOK OF FIVE RINGS

*

it was raining, and the
train ride rather dull

so you tore up
my poems sending

the pieces scattering
into the autumn mud

festering in the fields,
dark, stagnant pools.

        but now it's april. and
        across the valley

        forget-me-nots

        are blooming in the
        frail morning mist.

*

i

attacked from all
sides,

my selfish heart
shows

perfect form,

almost
beautiful

        in its austere
        ingratitude.

ii

yes, i am preoccupied
with myself, my poems.

so your arrows do wound,
black and white feathered

and straight, your silence
even more carefully. but

        when you have finished,
        my flesh then wind-scattered
        and bright to the pale sun,

i will dance upon
the rocky cliffs,

above the raging
winter torrents,

and mock you.
mock you.

*

ni wa no sanshu no ki
naru suzu kakete yo hoi!

i

wait for me by the bridge
with the green water
that you love. tell them
you've gone to feed the
fishes and to weep.

when you throw bread upon the
water, they turn like fire.
we were both meant
to be poor and suffer.

ii

listen! can you hear the wind?
look! the mountains burn up!

oh, against the night and
the red sun coming,

i touch my finger
to your sky!

utsukushii
utsukushii

iii

koma ni mizu kuryo to
yute demashō yo!

iv

so we walked along the river
and gathered stones together.

and when i knelt to touch
the water with my hand,

did you turn? run?

v

   —would you like misoshiru?

   —yes, sukoshi.

   —kore de ii no?

   —yes, ii yo.

vi
when i was a boy in fowler,
ojī-chan would mystify me.

on sundays, he dressed in a black
suit and preached to his people;

but on saturday, i would peek
into the church and see him

on his hands and knees,
scrubbing the floors alone.

shigekawa sensei, ojī-chan,
you are my only teacher.

vii

hey listen! listen, you guys! so
it was third and goal, see, and it
was obvious they were gonna runa
28- or a 22- . . . it wasn't
no surprise or nothin'—and like, we
were up, man, up! okada sounded like he
was goin' outa his fuckin' mind screamin'
shit like 'you gotta kill his ass now!
kill his ass!!' and i was standin' like
this—'come on, you sonofabitch! come on!'
but hey, when they started that sweep, man,
that mother just picked up the guards, the
full back, the tight end—and it was, like—
'HERE COME THE TROJANS!!' shhhiiii . . . .

viii

to have dreamed of
a mountain,

mont-st. michel,
milton's room, monk
on fifty-second street,
cordelia now, or
felix, poor felix
randal, oh, is he dead
then, my duty all ended?

but you entered without
knocking—

    chika'ma!
    chika'ma!

you whispered . . .

bright blood splatters
against these frail white walls
until my guts ooze
to mingle with yours.

—kore de ii no?

—yes, ii yo.

(ii no?)

(ii yo.)

ix

white cranes rise
from winter tanbo
as the wind comes
to comfort me.

i walk through this
land, carrying my
bento and a book
of english poems.

when i come to a
place, we kneel,
and sing. *'odoma
bongiri bongiri
bon kara sakya orando . . .'*

this is how we
study
yeats, or the blues.

        white bird,
        my friend,
        fly . . .

x

i smell geh-geh on
my shirt while she
lies upon the mat,
staring into the sun.
'shino-chan?'
i count her tiny fingers
and blow
against her cheek.

    'listen. the third
    movement of the
    d major sonata
    is *andante* . . .'

but her eyes still follow
the wind
through the trees.

suddenly, she laughs,
and laughs. (yes,

you are my daughter,
aren't you?

xi

very simply stated, the point
is this: if we wish to know
the location, of, say, a *pion,*
we cannot at the same time
measure, with any precision,
its momentum, and vice versa.
so we have to decide which
we'd like to know. of course,

this is a simple fact about the
nature of human understanding.
nothing more. one shouldn't want
to call it a philosophy of life.

xii

from the bizen jar
in the corner,
take a dipper full
of water.

> *shino-chan?*
> *omizu wa?*

shino? where's the
kiku? (good girl!)

> *shinobu?*
> *naginata wa?*

now come on, shino-chan!
come on, muhka-muhka!

come on, shino-chan!
hora! rocky road!

xiii

i left you one last
persimmon.

a black crow came to
receive it.

now here are the leaves
i have brought for you,

> and these,
> and these,
> and these.

xiv

though i am broken
and the pieces hang to
dry in the sun, all pity
and regret are gone. i

     can see the slope
     of life's full
     circle
     turning slowly
     into the night.

yes, it's been a wild ride
and full of speculation.

yes, there's nothing left
but the waiting. here, then,

     is the fire
     of my life
     and my true
     spirit. i

give them to you
for you have loved me
long enough.

oningyōsama, whisper
softly into her ear,
how i am cruel and
heartless, breaking
you into a thousand
pieces that fly
into the sun. but

now i too can feel the
beauty of non-existence,
and the peace

     of your small hand
     pointing

     carelessly
     forever.

xv

when i must go,
i shall eat
a simple meal
with all our
spirits
living and dead.

they will dance
around the fire
and hang lanterns
along the path
where i walk.

as it gets dark,
would you leave
a small light on?

and wait for me
by the bridge
with the green
water
that you love, and

tell them, you've
gone to feed
the fishes,
and to weep.

*no ni wa nogiku no
hana zakari yo!*

                    *

black wind,
        must you be
        unkind?

black wind,
        look, even
        matsu sways!

        (my kite!
        (my kite!

black wind,
        does your love
        hang dead?

black wind,
        the mountains
        burn up!

oh, against the night
and the red sun
        coming,

        i touch my
        finger
        to your sky.

black wind,
black wind,

        utsukushii!
        utsukushii!

                    *

i

it was simply a
matter of

economics,
wasn't it?

arriving so late
at night,

naturally we
weren't dressed

properly, and
somewhat

faulty at speech,
literary tastes.

ii

since i was
a child,

the moon rose to
comfort me,

like an ancient
pine,

above that bright
and rolling water.

iii

i, the
baptised.

the an-
ointed.

    be still.
    be still.

iv

the woman dances
upon the mountain

for the boy who
doesn't want to die

in santa monica.
"oh, there is no shame!"

v

my father whispers
that they came from the

sea and cast their
fishes
across the hot sand,
singing.

    ei ya sa!
    ei ya sa!

vi

patience.
patience.

mercedes benz.

vii

in a thousand
years i shall

have known them
all and found

a boring,
retroactive
salvation.

now, close your
eyes, and sleep.

my child, my
lovely one.

*

i

this is a
rake.

and this,
a broom.

and this, a
jar

of water.

i give them
to you.

ii

could i have some
chocolate

with almonds, a song
without words?

iii

in the morning, i
am a cloud

in the evening, i
return as rain.

and this is how
i love you.

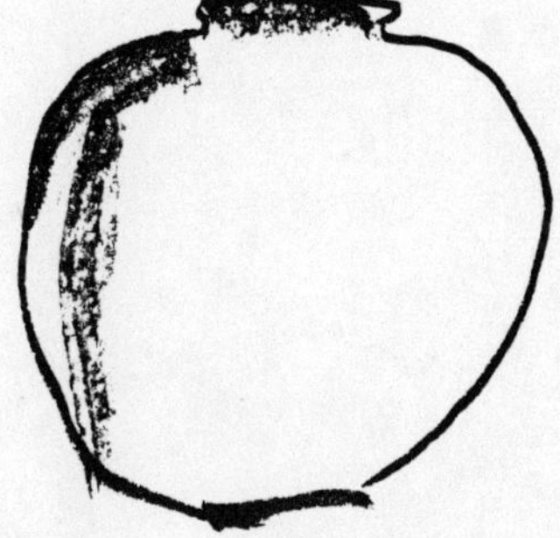

i've been taught to expect a certain precision
in human relationships. in aesthetic terms,
this means that one can't expect to have both
beauty and comfort. i assume you understand.

*he thought he saw in his
arrogance some long
forgotten warrior prince.*

i'd say this: you have no compassion. you are
devoid of human feeling. a poem or a tamba jar
would have more substance to you than a person
of flesh and blood. you never loved me, but
rather an image, a reflection of your own desire
for a sense of place in an indifferent universe.

*

oh, would you drink
my blood and
have my child,
and carry it up
the mountain

to pray?

or should i be the
ancestor of no one,
languishing in time,
dying, very properly,
alone, as i've

been taught?

*

as time draws near,
i become
impatient. i buy
flowers

impulsively, and
turn them

in their vases
until they die.

*

but when i heard the
news, i prowled

the streets for
hours, looking

for a price low enough
for a true believer.

    open the door! quickly!
    it is i, david, your king!

*

you'll enter the world
in a kaiser

hospital. a point
of entry

sufficiently ironic
for the daughter

    of an
    albatross.

    b. 2 june 1944
    camp 1
    poston, arizona

*

they had your name
taped to

that plastic thing
you were

lying in.
SHINOBU TANAKA

when they asked me
what it meant,

i said: 'the plum tree
who was a poet.'

*

the bamboo vase in
the dining room

will crack soon, the
climate in

california be-
ing inappropriate.

*

what? mercutio
and lady capulet?

i gasped,
startled at

my wild,
beating heart.

*

i

first draw a
circle,

    though not too
    perfectly.

yes. that's right.
(well, very good!)

ii

so humboldt defined
a world.

    let us call it
    W_1.

iii
li po swaggered
through another

    rich with cheap wine
    and plum blossoms.

    let us call it
    W_2.

iv

do you really think
there could have been

    a world
    full of white
    whales, ishmaels?

    W_3?

v

i think i'd really
rather be a

    red cross knight
    pricking merrily
    across the plains

    of W_4.

vi

sōtatsu did, in fact,
assume the historicity

    of heian elegance.
    (or was it simply

    a revolt
    against W_5?)

xiv

R2: $-(W^* \& W^t)$

> R2 is true.
> probably R2.
> necessarily R2.
> ought R2.
> shall R2.
> for the real world.
> for any universe
> of possible worlds.

naite matsu yori
no ni dete ojyare yo hoi.

xv

i stepped outside
the circle,

and

fell into the
quiet rhythms

of your life.

caught in a moment,
was i

a semantic anomaly
or
simply ungrammatical?

xvi

this is the end,
isn't it?

please do wait.
i'll boil water.

xvii

my dying chrysanthemum,
how much more lovelier

now than fresh and so
full of life.

here is W^n.
my newest world.

and this, R3: (u&-u)
where

u = n v r.

xviii

itogiku.

i could write
forever

and not be
understood

by
anyone.

xix

but this is how
i'll love you.

    (10,000 years)

xx

∅

*

the two kiku in the
bathroom have

been dead for a month
... their stems,

their petals fragile
with age, but

elegant as they
casually

soar off into the
darkness together.

each morning, i brush
my teeth to

the rhythms of their
dance. when they're

through, i'll burn them.

*

lo, the clown bruised
before you in one last
midnight performance.

  "for a bottle of
  le montrachet
  i'd do *any*thing!"

listen! that's his blood
oozing through
those tiny fractures.

  from mushin to
  modal logic.
  ghastly sight.
  isn't it? well,

oh, and now,
hermione . . .

*

"this is a sacred spear
with feathers," i explain,

"a recent acquisition."
"it cost a fortune,"

mother says, smiling.

"then we were lucky
to have gotten it!"

our daughter cries.

"yes, yes," mother says,
"please come along, dear!"

i nod and turn and
straighten my tie

and stick my hands into
the pockets of my vest

still hearing him scream-
ing in my ears:

      "shinken shōbu!"

he taught me this:
intellectuals who turn

anti-intellectual
turn into facists.

      "only at dawn can one say
      the mountain is pure."

      "i know," she smiles.

      the sound of steel against
      the morning, the sacred bell.

                        *

la chapelle aux ronchamps.

i've been here many times,
creation of

photographs,
a child's mind.

          how could an atheist
          do such a thing?
          i demand, but like

pilate, will not stay
for an answer.

          into the fields,
          a boy runs laughing.

          'momoyama shino!'
          'momoyama shino!'

*

i'd heard you calling
for weeks

always in little whis-
pers, but

incessantly like
the wind.

then, early one
morning,

i arose and came to
you with-

out sighs, kisses—even
my lunch.

for days i cast my frail
line in-

to the crashing surf, but
caught no-

thing. it was then you sent
before

me, then blurry-eyed and
raging,

a pale orange sun, low o-
ver the

horizon and soft, softly
. . . oh when

they found me, i was float-
ing and

purple bag-like, awful to
behold.

would you have loved me then,
and kissed my smiling face?

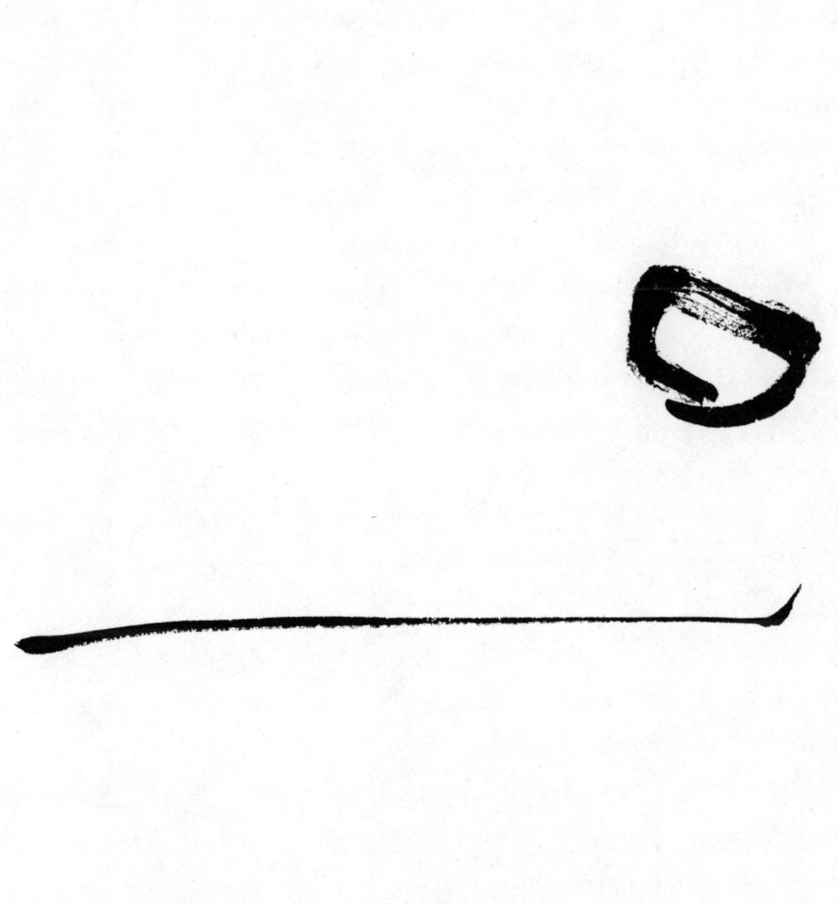

*

i

the clouds are
young today.

above the lake,
little boys fly

     paper airplanes,
     casually
     dropping them

     like
     blossoms

upon the blue sea.

ii

on a clear night,
when there is no
wind, you can hear

them singing
as they die.

still, they do
not complain.

iii

am i
your
teacher?

*

when i get sad,
i beat my drum

and see my
troubles soar

into the
sun, dropping

as small rain
across the

trees that swing
to the sound

of my feet
upon the

bright spring grass.
come,

horse, laugh!

come,
horse, sing!

my drum, my drum,
my drum!

*

wrist-wrestling
in a bar.

it's not
awfully
dignified.

but let's —um—
try again—

only, more
leisurely,

with grace.

                    *

i

i saw you pacing the
sea at dawn.

            here! blue irises from
            a mountain village.

yes, i suppose they could remind
one of red lips and death, but . . .

            please wait, won't you?
            i'll boil water.

ii

i've held your soft
crackled glaze,
kissing the tired
clay beneath,
        still proud,
        still defiant.

and i must have felt
your hands, slipping
through my fingers,

one final breath
pulled free with
relief, a laugh.

            now, for love,
            with
            merchants' daughters.

iii

they say you've taken a
japanese name, a wife.

well, being sansei, i
do understand.

        could we
        have coffee
        some day?

*

down this
        path (be
        careful yo)

listen,

        water flowing
        across the tanbo.

shhhhhhh,

        is that
        the moon?

hey,

        where's the
        rabbit! (oh-oh!

        wait here
        wait here

                    *

i crouch against
dry susuki,

        eating musubi,
        drinking coke.

god, if you
should find me . . . !

*

daikon

    (large, white)

floating there,
trying hard

    to rot.

let me take
your picture.

'click!'

(leica MD-4)

*

in the light of a
winter moon,

i hacked off your hair
with my sword.

now you are only a
farmer's boy.

     look! over there!
     the east ranges!

was it then you heard
your daughter weeping?
his moaning flute?

     embrace the blood-stained
     snow!
     kiss the black wind!

this strand of hair,
brave men's dreams.

*

i

there is none. pitched
into the abyss,
your arrogance tipping
dew-like
the sleeping mourning blade.

       betty cuts her onions
       afraid lest she should weep.

ii

each day i rebuild
your shrine

to the sound of the
temple bell.

       i chase away the butterflies
       and ask the flowers
       not to bloom so brightly.

now i take up stones
your feet have trod,

       and wash away
       the blood.

iii

here is a fish of clay,
dinner for my child,

a flower of sand,
my wife.

if you chain me to the sun,
i'll plow the sky,

and gold will fill your coffers.
(alas! the tinkling poet!)

iv
i am the moss
clinging to your roof,
your stones, the ancient bell.

i, the owl, standing
watch by night,

the pretty nightengale.

v

later that afternoon, they heard the
kettle begin to boil in the

middle room. when they looked, they saw
you kneeling beside the fire,

burning my poems. when you had finished,
your hair then wind-swept and pale

to the orange sun, you spooned my ashes
into a bowl, and drank them . . .

vi

beneath a crescent moon, your ox-man
kills his ox to feed his son,

and sells his women to your husband,
crying:

> *ei ya sa!*
> *ei ya sa!*

vii

i sat beside
the river,

and watched
a boy

fishing, or
his friend.

viii

now it is autumn. the momiji
are turning and i must leave

one last message for my daughter:
'though your father was a poet,

please become a mathematician,
untouched by beauty, reverence

or deceit. in the ideal realm of pure
possibility, we shall find our hope.'

*

the chinese jar in
shino's room,

sits, clay-crude
and brown

and dripping ash

against a wall of
winter white.

a farmer must have
sold it—for food,

perhaps, or new seeds;
its maker, long dead.

late at night, i
pace the floor.

'is this enough?'
i wonder.

*

when it is cold
and the rain

softly falling,
i want to fold

you into my arms,
and stand beneath

the ancient pine,
and dance, dance

to the nodding
of the leaves.

    my child, my
    lovely one.

*

now you put your
head on

my shoulder
and go

*'nen-ne-ne!
nen-ne-ne!'*

                    *

as soon as it was dark, you
began wandering through the

house, looking out the windows
for the moon. 'mune?' 'mune?'

you called, much too softly.
'shino,' i said, 'the moon

can't hear you.' angry, you
grabbed my hand, demanding

we look together. still, it
was no use. hours later,

after you'd cried yourself to
sleep, the moon came laughing

through your window. 'here i
am, shinobu-chan, kimashita yo!'

*

gohan on the blue chinese
carpet.

shino no ato.

*

when you sit, you often
become bored,

so you ask for things.
you say, 'be-ah,' and

your mother brings your
bear. 'blan-ki'

and she brings your blue
blanket. 'mo-mo'

and she brings your book.
shinobu-chan!

don't you realize how
silly you look

sitting there, holding
your bear, your blanket,

your book, your brush . . .?

one of these days you're
going to fall in

and go — *PA—CHONG!!* all gan!

*

this morning we heard you
talking to someone, so

we got out of bed and peeked
into your room. you

were standing in your crib,
saying, 'hi!' 'hi!'

to the purple iris
in the bamboo vase.

*

you stood before me
with your fan

extended, then lowered
your hips slightly,

turning slowly to the
beat of fue

and drums. you did this
over and over,

until you became dizzy
and fell on your back.

but in my mind's eye,
i could see you

going down to the sea
to gather salt.

and then, forgetting
yourself for a

moment, dancing
beneath

the vast heavens, for
the spirit of the

sun, of stones, pine, and
even the black wind.

                    *

'look, shino-chan!
saba!' and before

i could stop you,
you'd kissed one

on the nose.
'hi, fuwish!'

*

once there was an old
man and an

old woman. all day
long, he goes

into the forest to
gather wood

while she kneels beside
the fire, waiting

for the man she loves.

*

born between the year
of the battered

morgan and the gucci
purse, you turn

the pages of all our
books, looking for

shigaraki jars and
old bizen. should

you continue on to
develop an

interest in either
mendelssohn or

the japanese dance,
people would say

you were born unlucky
and bring you gifts.

> '. . . hoping you'll grow up to be
> a beautiful little fool, darling!'

*

i

they walk along
the water,

    wife and mistress
    together.

upon the damp
grass, dogs run
shrouded in fog.

    turn your collar
    against the cold,

    laughter, barking, waves
    lapping in the wind.

ii

should i, like some
happy gibbon,

    come screaming
    through the sky?

(oh, you're spoilt silly,
aren't you, child!)

    then i'll drown, drunk,
    with the red sun

    clutched in a tiny,
    sweating hand.

*

i

can you see the
sun against
my office window?

    can you taste this
    instant
    freeze-dried coffee?

look, my cuff
is frayed.

oh, today, today, today.

ii

lo the sparrow, brown
against your silence.
the pale chrysanthemum
turning brown.

and i walk upon
the earth

until my lungs,
my stout heart

burst: browning
grade 3, 12-gauge
field gun. 45

    rounds per minute.

iii

tonight i moved the
stones inside

my garden and raked
away the leaves.

    agnus dei, qui tollis
    peccata mundi.

    swish!
    swish!
    swish!

iv

i'll sail my boat
against the sea

at 0900 hours,
to be broken, burned.

though the burn unit
won't accept me,

the war should go on,
and children smile

in tōkyō, vail,
afghanistan.

please, please,
my darlings,

live all you can!

v

my kimono colors,
my obi colors,
        float upon the
        oil slick

blue oxford
broadcloth,

torn tweeds and
paisley

        frail upon the
        oil slick water.

do not call this the
death of intellect.

simply unbutton my
collar.

vi

here i am again,
the militant

butterfly

lately emerged
from a

corporate pumpkin
worm, and

still, still oozing
bright vermilion,

my duty all ended.

vii

the typist has a
blue *selectric*

blithely produced in
prague, and i

have promised to save
my tweeds

with chinese patches
on the arms. so

this should be a
relatively just

distribution of
happiness

ceteris paribus,

for we both loved
the dying chrysanthemum
best of all.

*

i watered the rocks
in the front garden.

they were thirsty,
but longed

for purity even more.
the two in the

back, however,
died long ago.

one from sadness, the
other from

simple neglect. i know.

*

i want to make you
breakfast.

raisin muffins on
gray shino

garnished with a
fern from

the window box. and
coffee. my

famous blend of mocha
java and dark french.

if you like, you could
bring flowers.

the vase is egg shell
stoneware—from gump's.

*

tonight the stripers
are up by grimes

     but i'm here,
     by habit.

a month ago,
i waited, trembling,

     as your strong brute
     bodies moved beneath

     the black water,

     quietly, like the spirits
     of ancient warriors.

nothing happened.

though i would
have killed you
if i could,

     smashing your skulls
     against the rocks

     until the blood oozed
     and i could eat that

     flesh, raw, with rice.

you're almost safe now,
and there's only me again.

     i wish you well.
     kiotsukete ne.

                    *

i

then, finally, the plum
flowers so beautiful,

you could not bear to
see them, you, standing

beneath the shadows,
small and trembling.

and when you knelt
to touch the water
with your hand,
i came to you
without knocking.

                (did you turn?
                stand?)

ii

on a clear spring night
at numazu beach,

a fisherman was suddenly
smothered by a

robe of celestial
feathers, and

that face, laughing
above the bright

and rolling water. i, a
poor fisherman,

and you, whoever you are.

iii

should my eyes remind
you of a

certain bach violin
sonata,

the warm rain would wet
your hair, and

cherry blossoms cling to you.
oh, it'd be

a thousand-year-old lie,
rare, and

almost lovely in its
mindless arrogance.

iv

were we vulgar, you'd have
brought me takuan

on gray shino, and i'd have
made you ochazuke.

um. but we were not.

v

and i said: 'once there
was an old man

and an old woman . . .'
'yes,' you said,

'and all day long, he
goes into the

forest to gather wood,
while she kneels

beside the fire, waiting
for the man she loves.'

vi

you drew a circle on
the window of your

white alfetta. 'our
passion!' you smiled.

and we laughed, for it
was very, very

funny, and very,
very sad—

our passion . . .

vii

certain god-like spaces
fill your garden.

the rocks lie dumb. and
even crickets

bow in awe of you. i know.

viii

you were late again.
so i talked

about music. mendels–
sohn. we seemed

bored. when you left,
there was lipstick

on a white
porcelin cup.

ix

it must've been august
in california.

too warm for anything
really elegant.

only bluegills,
and catfish.

X

i'll walk across the
grain-ripe tanbo,

or dance, dance
to the beating

of the drum . . .

xi

there is a platform
at tōkyō eki.

you can buy
candy there.

    chocolate,
    with almonds.

xii

i left you
one last
persimmon.

yesterday,
a black crow
came
to receive it.

and here are
the leaves
i have
brought
for you.

     and these
     and these
     and these

xiii

it was then you sent before him,
then blurry-eyed and raging,

a pale orange sun, low over
the horizon, and soft, softly . . .

xiv

run, run to the lake
where you were young!

JAPAN JAPAN

(what have you done
to me?

do you lie awake at night,
dreaming of a mountain, japan?

yes.

now it's your turn.
come.

see tamalpais. and
die.

xv

my study has very few
books, but i can feel

>the autumn moon
>as i lie

>upon my mat,
>and the same

sonata for harpsichord
and viol da gamba,

esther phillips.
could you wait

a moment for i must consider
von humboldt's magic circles,
or a cat named jeoffrey.

>*(ocha iru no?*

xvi

sacramento is lovely in
the rain. if you

are very quiet, you can
hear voices

crying in the wilderness.

my kite!
my kite!

xvii

after kendō, i feel
whole again.

pure again. but still,
it frightens me.

sato imo. ko-bizen.

xviii

thursday shopping:

    —chicken
    —butter
    —kaki
    —tōfu
    —brie
    —takuan (for shino-chan

and, um, let's see . . . a case
of freemark abbey *bosché*.

xix

he said: 'you must want to
kill without regret

or find no freedom here.'
'yes,' i said. 'i know.'

XX

cricket!
cricket!

xxi

i can't sleep.

so i'll make myself
some coffee

and listen to
leonard rose.

and when morning
comes, put

flowers in the
vase you loved.

xxii

in california,
we are protected

     from the seasons.
     we feel no pain.

poetry is a commodity,
and love, casual,

     like rain,
     like ume no hana.

the hum of traffic
on interstate five.

     whine of the
     fuel-injected porsche.

*

five musubi
left lying
in the spring snow.

          an offering
          to the gods.

would you weep
to know

i am still traveling
over
the mountain plains?

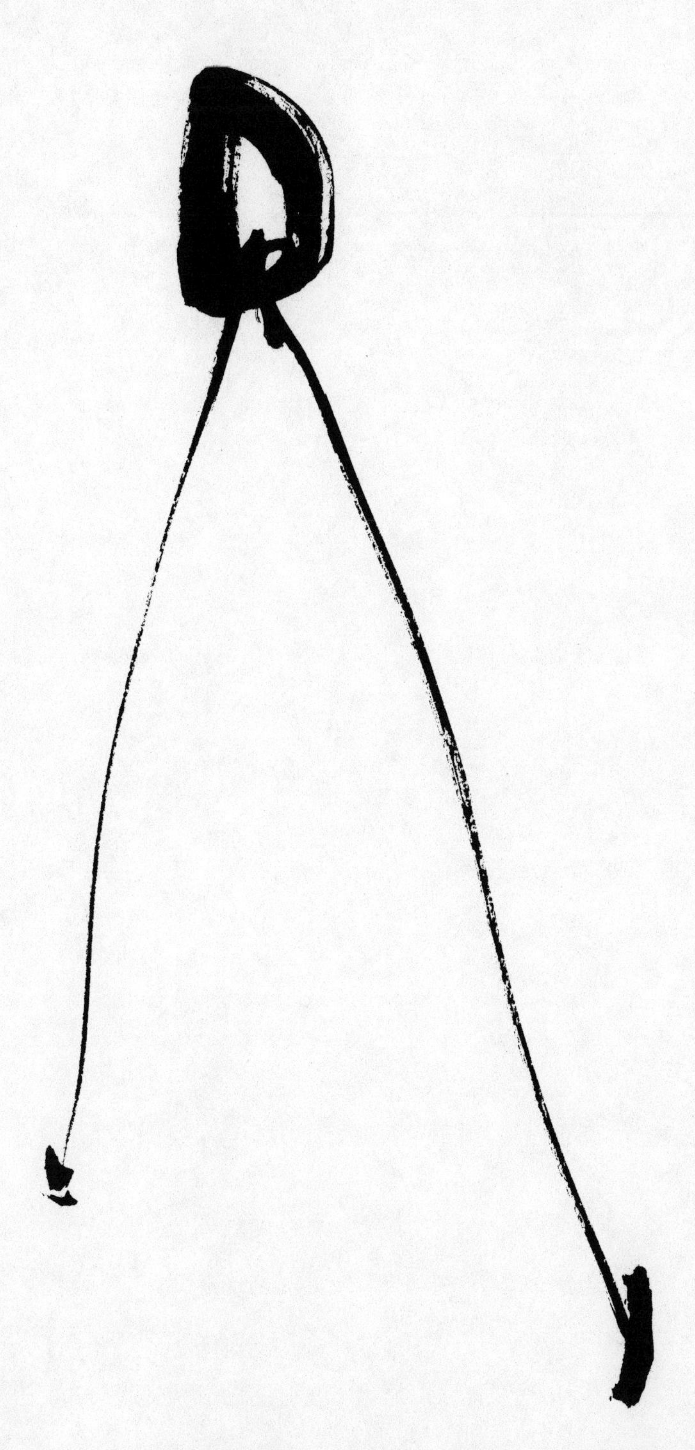

APPENDIX A

*Hietsuki Bushi**

niwa no sanshu no ki	on to the wild ash tree
naru suzu kakete yo hoi!	i will put a bell, yo hoi!
suzu no naru to kya	when it jingles,
dete ojyare yo.	you come out, yo.
suzu no naru to kya	when it jingles, jingles,
nanto yute demasho yo hoi!	for what excuse shall i come,
koma ni mizu kuryo to	for watering the horse,
yute demasho yo.	i'll come out, yo.
naite matsu yori	if you must wait weeping,
no ni dete ojyare yo hoi!	go into the fields.
no ni wa nogiku no	there the field chrysanthemum
hana zakari yo!	are blooming, yo.

*English translations for the first two verses from Ryutaro Hattori (ed.)
Japanese Folk Songs, Japan Times: Tokyo, 1950.

APPENDIX B

But in the next instant, when he asked himself what it was he had read,
there was nothing. There was so much nothing, it was funny. He felt only
that he had read a lot and read it eagerly. Sanshiro was struck with
admiration for Yojiro's literary skill.

—Natsume Sōseki
SANSHIRO

NOTES

Every attempt has been made to keep the number of Japanese words and expressions to a minimum. However, the everyday language of even monolingual Sansei like myself cannot be adequately represented without some Japanese expressions though it must be borne in mind that their significance is grounded in a distinctly Japanese-American *Lebensform*. The following translations are literal. No attempt will be made to explain why any particular word or phrase is used since this can be determined from the context.

There are a few general definitions that might be best given here at the beginning. Japanese-Americans usually refer to themselves generationally: *Issei, the first generation to come from Japan, Nisei, the first generation born abroad, Sansei, the third generation, or the second born abroad.* The title of the poem refers to Shino ware, a type of thickly glazed Japanese pottery. It is also homophonous with the shortened form of my daughter's name, *Shinobu,* which means to endure quietly. Shino was born in December of 1976.

The Shino Suite was begun in 1972 and was essentially complete by 1979. It is part of a series which includes the two collections of opus 1 and the three pieces of opus 3.

3   *spring*
4   *on style*
5   *boku no michi*: my path (way).
      This poem is structured around *Hietsuki Bushi,* an old Japanese folk song (see Appendix A). All of the italicized sections are from this song.
      utsukushii: beautiful, lovely.
6   'would you like misoshiru?': this dialogue goes:
      —would you like some miso soup?
      —yes, a little.
      —is this enough?
      —yes.
      oji-chan: grandpa.
      sensei: a general term usually referring to teachers, masters of various professions and arts, etc. My grandfather was a Christian minister.
7   chika'ma': a technical expression from Japanese fencing which is short for *chikai maai* referring to the close interval between opponents.
8   tanbo: rice field.
      bento: lunch.
      "*odoma bongiri. . .*": from *Itsuki no Komoriuta,* a Japanese folk song.

10   bizen: a type of old unglazed Japanese pottery.
       omizu: water.
       kiku: chrysanthemum.
       naginata: literally, 'long sword.' A single-edged blade attached to a
               spear-like pole. The use of this weapon has developed
               into a martial art practiced primarily by women. Both of
               my grandmothers were trained in naginata.
11   oningyōsama: the speaker is addressing a doll.
13   *across the tanbo wind blows*
       matsu: Japanese pine.
14   *santa monica beach sleep*
17   *this*
22   fragment from "i hate my wife," a poem first published in *Gidra*
               (1968).
23   tamba: a type of traditional Japanese folk pottery.
27   *yamamba:* old woman of the mountain.
28   *rebirth*
29   *expecting*
30   *kaiser*
31   *and then i went to coffee*
32   *bamboo*
33   *michael smuin's romeo and juliet*
37   *hermeneutics:* the science of interpretation.
39   takuan: pickled white radish.
42   itogiku: commonly called a 'spider mum.'
43   *kiku*
44   *pierrot*
45   *the sacred spear*
       shinken shōbu: 'let's duel with live swords!'
46   *ronchamps*
       momoyama shino: refers to the Shino ware of the Momoyama
               period (1568-1603) of Japanese history when
               Shino was at its most elegant.
47   *to the 5 lb. 4 oz. red-tail perch*
51   *the lake near tsuchiura:* a city in Ibaragi-ken situated near a lake
               where very young suicide pilots were trained.
52   *tohoku taiko*
       tohoku: northern region of Japan.
       taiko: drum.
53   *ta-san's two o'clock game.*
54   *karatsu bowl with iris:* a type of Japanese pottery originally
               developed by Korean potters who were often
               nothing more than highly-valued slaves to the
               Japanese.
56   *on a late summer night when semi can be heard to sing*
       semi: cicada.

57   *ibaragi bento*
     susuki: pampas grass.
     musubi: rice ball.
58   *winter lotus pond*
     daikon: long white radish.
59   *disguise*
63   *aubade*
65   momiji: Japanese maple.
66   *for dr. stephen s.n. liu*
67   *oimatsu*
68   *at last i am your father*
69   *moon viewing*
     kimashita yo: 'I've come!'
70   *after a famous poem by bashō*
     gohan: cooked rice.
     shino no ato: Shino's aftermath.
71   *unchi*
72   *the purple iris*
73   *shino no odori:* Shino's dance.
74   *on a summer afternoon at senator fish*
     saba: mackerel.
75   *story*
76   *destiny*
     shigaraki: a type of unglazed Japanese pottery.
77   *english bay*
81   *butterfly*
85   *279 munroe*
86   *it'll have to do*
87   *while night fishing at bryte's bend*
     kiotsukete ne: 'be careful, won't you?'
88   *solo suite in d major*
91   ochazuke: tea over rice.
98   tōkyo eki: the main train station in Tōkyō.
101 tamalpais: a mountain overlooking San Francisco Bay.
102 'ocha iru no?': 'would you like some tea?'
104 kendō: the art of Japanese fencing.
     sato imo: taro root.
105 tōfu: soy bean curd.
     kaki: persimmon.
109 ume no hana: plum blossoms.
110 *tangerine leaves*

A WORD OF THANKS

This was the most difficult section of all to write. As I began to list all of the persons who might properly be thanked for directly or indirectly helping me, the task became endless. So what I've decided to do is to say thank you to you all, and hope that simply seeing *Shino* published will be sufficient reward for your efforts. I should, however, give special credit to a few people who were necessary for bringing her out of the xerox circuit into her present form. My first word of thanks goes to Dr. Stephen S. N. Liu who initially proposed publication to my kind editor, Joseph Bruchac III. Then there is my brother, Mark Stephen Tanaka, who literally supported me during two important periods. And my parents, William S. and Mari Tanaka, who allowed me to give my life to poetry. Finally, of course, Shinobu, my daughter, and that face, laughing, above the bright and rolling water. My thanks. My thanks.

Calligraphy by Paul Motoyoshi, Sr. Woodcut of the Bizen jar named 'Hashihime' by Shinya Tomine. All other illustrations by the author.

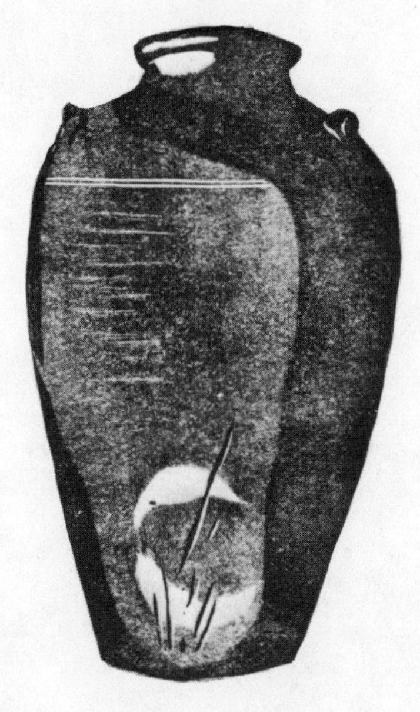

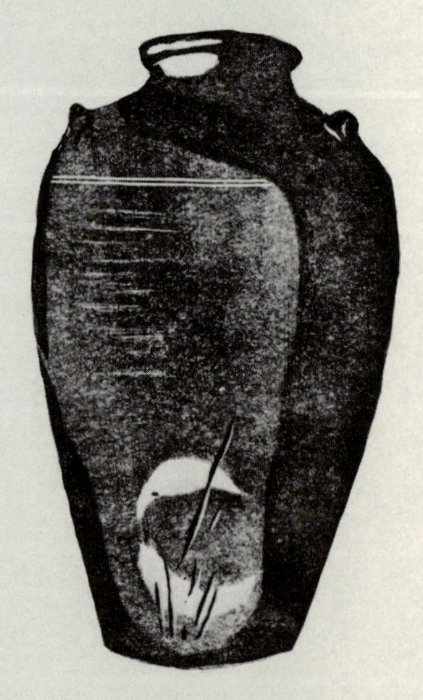